# *Jennifer Lopez*

Julia Holt

PURCHASED THROUGH
MOFFAT FAMILY
FUND

D1158897

Published in association with Tॖ ॗॗॖॖ Agency

## Hodder & Stoughton

A MEMBER OF THE HODDER HEADLINE GROUP

**Acknowledgements**
*Cover: © All Action*

*Photos: p. 2 © Alpha; p. 7 © The Ronald Grant Archive; pp. 11, 18 © The Kobal Collection; pp. 13, 23 © AP Photos; pp. 20, 24 © All Action.*

Every effort has been made to trace copyright holders of material reproduced in this book. Any rights not acknowledged will be acknowledged in subsequent printings if notice is given to the publisher.

Orders: please contact Bookpoint Ltd, 130 Milton Park, Abingdon, Oxon OX14 4SB. Telephone: (44) 01235 827720, Fax: (44) 01235 400454. Lines are open from 9.00 – 6.00, Monday to Saturday, with a 24 hour message answering service. You can also order through our website www.hodderheadline.co.uk

*British Library Cataloguing in Publication Data*
A catalogue record for this title is available from The British Library

ISBN 0 340 84885 5

First published 2002
Impression number     10 9 8 7 6 5 4 3 2
Year                            2007  2006  2005  2004

Copyright © 2002 Julia Holt

Typeset by SX Composing DTP, Rayleigh, Essex.
Printed in Great Britain for Hodder & Stoughton Educational, a division of Hodder Headline, 338 Euston Road, London NW1 3BH by CIP Bath.

# Contents

# 1    Introduction

Against all the odds
Jennifer Lopez is a big star.
She is not blonde.
She is not thin.
She has Latin looks
and she comes from the Bronx.
This is a very tough part of New York.

Jennifer's parents came to New York
from Puerto Rico.
Her dad worked in computers.
Her mum was a teacher in a Catholic school.
The family lived in a small flat.
Jennifer was born on 24 July 1970.
She is the middle one of three girls.

Jennifer Lopez has come a long way since her days in the Bronx.

Jennifer's Mum loved musical films.
She sat with her girls
and watched musicals on TV.
But there were very few Puerto Rican stars
for the girls to look up to.
So they pretended to be Charlie's Angels.

There was always music playing in the flat.
They listened to rap and soul.
Each weekend
the three girls went to dance classes.
Jennifer wanted to be a dancer in films.
Today Lynda is a DJ,
Leslie is a music teacher
and Jennifer is a music and film star.
Music is very important to all of them.

# 2   First Steps

When she was 13 years old,
Jennifer had a brush with death.
A truck hit her mum's car.
Jennifer was saved
because she was bending down
tying her shoelace at the time.
But she did get a broken nose.
Today her nose is flat
but she likes it that way.

At 15 years old
Jennifer got her first real boyfriend.
They were together for nine years.
His name was David.
But Jennifer didn't want to settle down.

At first she wanted to be a hairdresser.
She went to college in New York.
But she soon dropped out.
She wanted to be a dancer.
Her parents were not happy.

Jennifer wanted to work in films.
But she didn't know how to get into film work.
There were not many
Latin dancers to help her.

Every day she went on the number six train
to dance classes in New York.
She also tried to get work.
She went to lots of auditions.
Soon she got work dancing in pop videos.
Each job was better than the last.
She danced in Japan
and she toured with musical shows.

# 3  Changing Fortunes

In 1990, Jennifer got her big break in LA.
She went to an audition for a new TV show.
It was called *In Living Color*.
They weren't looking for
all-American blondes.
Jennifer was chosen
to be one of the five dancers.

There was lots of new talent in the show
including a young Jim Carrey.
The show was a big success.
It went out twice a week for four years.
For the first time in her life
Jennifer had some money.
She took acting classes and fitness training.
Jennifer knew she could do better.

Jennifer chose an agent
to help her find work.
She picked the same one as Jim Carrey.
Her agent found her work on other TV shows.
But she didn't want a career in TV.
She wanted to work in films.

Luckily Jennifer was
in the right place at the right time.
Hollywood was learning from the internet
that people didn't want to see
blonde actresses all the time.
So Hollywood started to look for Latin actresses.

In 1995, Jennifer was asked to play a cop
in the film *Money Train*.
It was not a big success, but it was a start.
In the next two years
she made four more films.

Jennifer's career was taking off.
But her personal life was not.
Jennifer and David split up
after nine years together.

Jennifer plays a New York cop in *Money Train*.

In 1997, Jennifer went to Florida
to make the film *Blood and Wine*.
One night she went out for a Cuban meal.
She fell in love
with one of the Cuban waiters.
His name was Ojani.

Jennifer told her friend
'That's the man I'm going to marry,'
and she was right.
One year later, on 22 February, 1997
they were married.

Jennifer hired someone to help plan
the wedding.
Jennifer and Ojani were married
at a friend's house in front of 200 people.
Then they went to the beach
for a one-week honeymoon.

# 4    *Out of Sight*

After her short honeymoon
Jennifer went back to work.
She wanted to make a record.
But first she had another film to make.

She was chosen
to star in a film with George Clooney.
It was called *Out Of Sight*.
He plays a bank robber and she plays a cop.
They fall in love.

When the film came out in June 1998
it was a big success.
Jennifer was now a box office star.

She was named as one of the
50 most beautiful women in the world.
But, three months after her wedding,
her marriage was falling apart.

Jennifer with George Clooney in *Out of Sight*.

# 5   Jennifer and Puff Daddy

Jennifer was seen out with Puff Daddy.
She was in one of his music videos.
Puff Daddy was not just a rap star,
he was also a millionaire business man.

He had a New York house worth $2.5 million.
He was everything that Ojani was not
and he helped Jennifer to make a record.

In March 1998,
Jennifer and Ojani divorced.
But she said that she was
just good friends with Puff Daddy.
He made Hollywood nervous
because he was a gangster rapper.
It was a stressful year for Jennifer.

Jennifer with Puff Daddy in 1999.

Nineteen ninety-nine was
a better year for Jennifer.
Puff Daddy helped her
to make her first album.
She called it *On the 6*.
This was the train that took her to New York
when she was younger.

The album was an instant hit.
She picked a good time
to make an album.
Latin music was very popular
and Ricky Martin had just become
a big Latin star.

Jennifer and Puff Daddy
kept their love a secret
until her twenty-ninth birthday in 1999.
Everyone ate pink birthday cake
as the two lovers kissed in a corner.

From that day on they were front page news.
There were photos of their clothes
and their parties in all the magazines.

# 6   The Cell

Towards the end of 1999
Jennifer made another film.
It was called *The Cell*.
She played a doctor who helps to catch
a serial killer.

Then Jennifer went back to New York
for Christmas.
On 26th December
Puff Daddy and Jennifer went to a club.
He was throwing money about.
Then he got into a fight.
It ended with three people getting shot.
Puff Daddy and Jennifer ran away.

The police stopped them
and they spent the night in jail.
Jennifer was cleared and sent home.
Puff Daddy was charged but later cleared.

Jennifer stuck by him.
But the pressure was too much.
They split up.
They told the press about the split
on Valentine's Day 2000.

# 7   A Fresh Start

Jennifer moved on.
Soon she had a new boyfriend.
He was a dancer called Cris Judd.
From November 2000
they were hardly ever apart.

Jennifer also had a new film to work on.
It was a comedy called *The Wedding Planner*.
Jennifer plays a career woman.
Her job is to plan weddings.
But she falls in love with the groom
of a wedding that she is working on.

Jennifer stars with Matthew McConaughey in *The Wedding Planner*.

For two weeks in January 2001
*The Wedding Planner* was the Number 1 film
in the movie charts
and her new album was the Number 1 album
in the music charts.
It was called *J. Lo*.

Jennifer was the first woman in history
to top both charts at the same time.

Jennifer is both a film and music chart-topper.

Jennifer's next film was a thriller.
It was called *Angel Eyes*.
Again, Jennifer plays an LA cop.
She has a tragic past.
One day she meets a man.
His family were killed in a car crash.
He has lost everything.
The man saves the cop's life.
They fall in love.
But they both have to deal with
their own tragedy.
The film came out in May 2001.

# 8    Success Story

For her next film Jennifer had to learn
a new way of fighting.
It was called Krav Maga.
Jennifer plays a woman
who marries a violent man.
The film is called *Enough*.
In the film the woman has to fight
for her life.

Cris was with Jennifer on the set
and the papers were full of photos of them.
Cris spent his life savings
on a ring for Jennifer.
Then, in September 2001,
they tied the knot.
They were married at sunset
in a big tent in the mountains,
just outside LA.

Jennifer and Cris on their wedding day.

Ever since she was a little girl
Jennifer Lopez has wanted
to sing, dance and act.
She has proved that she can do all three.
She has someone to do her make-up.
Someone to choose her clothes.
Someone to do her hair.
Someone to keep her fit.
She even has someone
to look after her eyebrows!

Jennifer Lopez doesn't have to dream anymore
It seems that she has everything.

Jennifer Lopez is one of Hollywood's biggest stars.
She even has her own 'J.Lo' clothing range
with Andy Hilfiger.

# Jennifer's Films

---

*Money Train* 1995

*My Family* 1995

*Jack* 1996

*Blood and Wine* 1997

*Anaconda* 1997

*Out of Sight* 1998

*Antz* 1998

*The Cell* 1999

*The Wedding Planner* 2000

*Angel Eyes* 2001

*Enough* 2002